MEDITATIVE ORIGAMI

FINDING MINDFULNESS THROUGH COLORING & ORIGAMI

JOHN MONTROLL

DOVER PUBLICATIONS, INC.
MINEOLA, NEW YORK

Bibliographical Note

Meditative Origami: 10 Origami Models to Fold with Designs You Color, is a new work, first published by Dover Publications, Inc., in 2019. The images have been selected from these previously published Dover books: *Mehndi Designs: Traditional Henna Body Art* by Marty Noble (2004); *Arabesque Designs Coloring Book* by Nick Crossling (2008); *Seashell Patterns Coloring Book* by Jessica Mazurkiewicz (2011); *Magnificent Mehndi Designs Coloring Book* by Marty Noble (2015); *More Mystical Mandalas Coloring Book* by Alberta Hutchinson (2015); *Dream Birds Coloring Book* by Miryam Adatto (2016); *ESCAPES Mosaics Coloring Book* by Jessica Mazurkiewicz (2016); *BLISS Flowers Coloring Book: Your Passport to Calm* by Lindsey Boylan and Jessica Mazurkiewicz (2016); *BLISS Dream Coloring Book: Your Passport to Calm* by Miryam Adatto (2017); *BLISS Nature Coloring Book: Your Passport to Calm* by Jessica Mazurkiewicz (2018); and *Stunning Succulents Coloring Book* by Jessica Mazurkiewicz (2019).

International Standard Book Number

ISBN-13: 978-0-486-83743-7
ISBN-10: 0-486-83743-2

Manufactured in the United States by LSC Communications
83743201
www.doverpublications.com

2 4 6 8 10 9 7 5 3 1

2019

Introduction

Combining the art of paper folding with coloring, *Meditative Origami* can be your pathway to achieving mindfulness and relaxation. With each color you add, each fold you make, you are inspired to achieve a new level of peace and tranquility.

Origami is an ancient craft that can be used to enhance mindfulness and improve concentration as well as a practical tool to let go of self-judgment and attain inner peace. With practice, origami may become a form of focused attention meditation: focusing on an object or task enables you to stabilize the mind and promote calmness.

Coloring is not only a means of personal expression, but it also allows you to concentrate and stay "in the moment." It is a simple, soothing way to relieve stress, as you use your own creativity to produce colorful designs. Your mind is free to focus on the task before you, not the stressors of the day.

You will find an assortment of black-and-white designs included in this book to be colored and used as origami paper. So carefully cut out the designs along the solid line, and provide your own embellishment with colored pencils or markers. Once your unique origami paper has been colored in, you are ready to explore new levels of mindfulness as you fold your own origami model.

A few things to note: the shading in the model diagrams refers to the colored side of the paper, so be sure to fold accordingly. Color in the entire design, right up to the edge. The origami diagrams conform to the internationally approved Yoshizawa-Randlett system. Within this book, there is valuable information included about the symbols and basic folds for the new origami enthusiast.

Contents

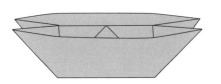

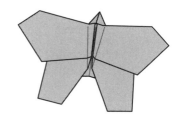

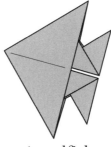

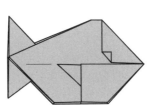

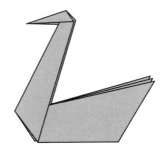

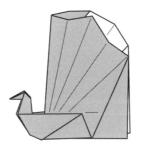

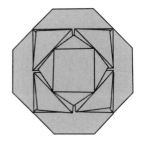

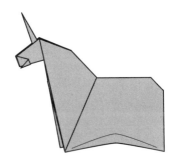

Symbols

Lines

— — — — — — — —   Valley fold, fold in front.

— · — · — · — · —   Mountain fold, fold behind.

————————   Crease line.

··············   X-ray or guide line.

Arrows

Fold in this direction.

Fold behind.

Unfold.

Fold and unfold.

Turn over.

Sink or three dimensional folding.

Place your finger between these layers.

Basic Folds

Squash Fold.

In a squash fold, some paper is opened and then made flat. The shaded arrow shows where to place your finger.

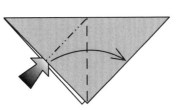
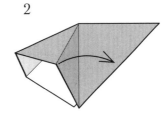
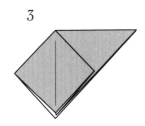

1   2   3

Squash-fold.   A 3D step.

Inside Reverse Fold.

In an inside reverse fold, some paper is folded between layers. Here are two examples.

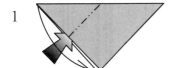

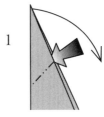

1   2   1   2

Reverse-fold.   Reverse-fold.

Outside Reverse Fold.

Much of the paper must be unfolded to make an outside reverse fold.

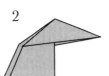
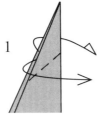

1   2

Outside-reverse-fold.

Crimp Fold.

A crimp fold is a combination of two reverse folds. Open the model slightly to form the crimp evenly on each side. Here are two examples.

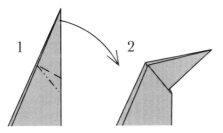
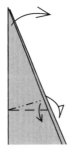
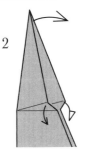
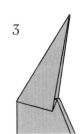

1   2   1   2   3

Crimp-fold.   Crimp-fold.   A 3D step.

Catamaran

1

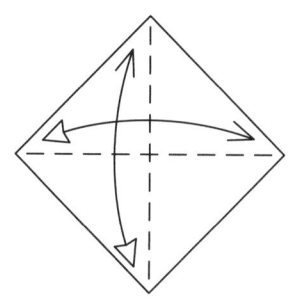

Fold and unfold.

2

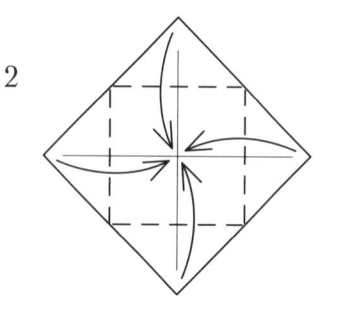

Fold to the center.

3

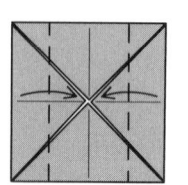

Fold to the center.

4

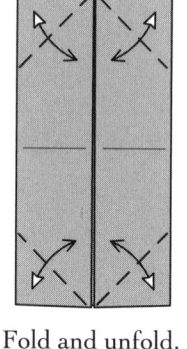

Fold and unfold.

5

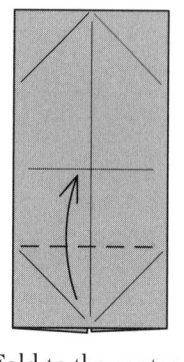

Fold to the center.

6

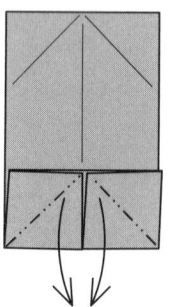

Make squash folds.

7

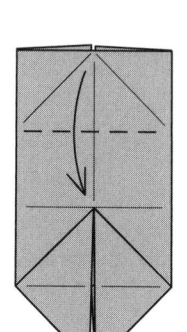

Repeat steps 5–6
on the top.

8

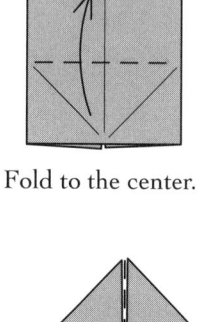

Fold in half and
rotate 90°.

9

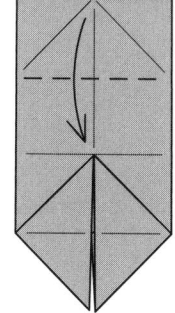

Spread to make the Catamaran
three-dimensional.

10

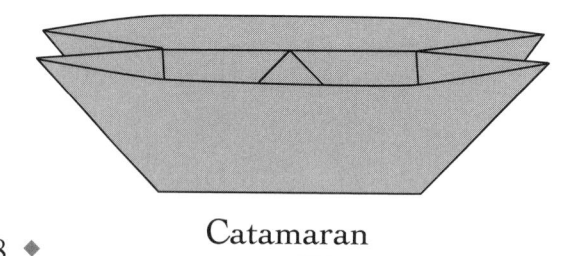

Catamaran

Butterfly

1
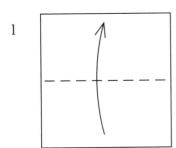

2

3
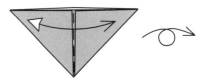

Fold and unfold.
Rotate 180°.

4
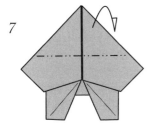

Fold to the center and
swing out from behind.

5
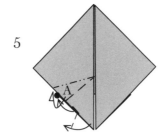

Note the dot is at a corner on the
hidden layer. Fold triangle A inside
so that the bold edge meets the dot.

6
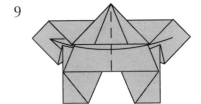

Repeat step 5
on the right.

7

8
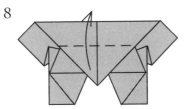

9

10
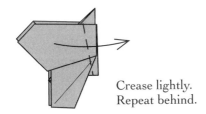

Crease lightly.
Repeat behind.

11
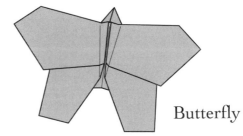

Butterfly

Angelfish

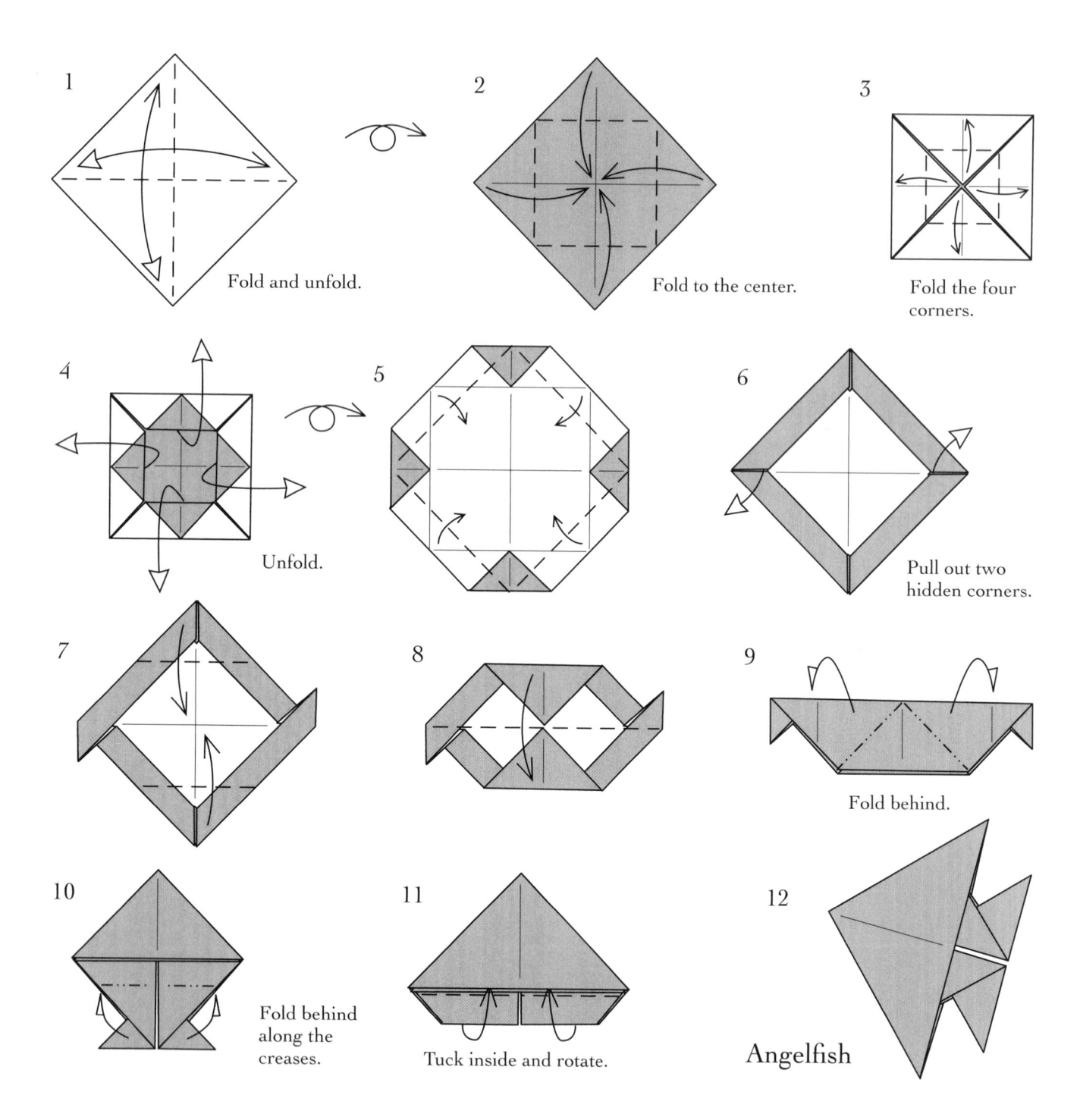

1

Fold and unfold.

2

Fold to the center.

3

Fold the four corners.

4

Unfold.

5

6

Pull out two hidden corners.

7

8

9

Fold behind.

10

Fold behind along the creases.

11

Tuck inside and rotate.

12

Angelfish

Fish

1
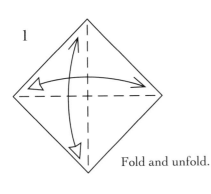
Fold and unfold.

2
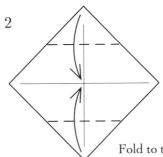
Fold to the center.

3
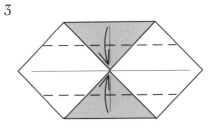
Fold to the center.

4
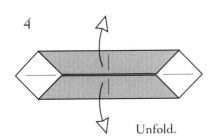
Unfold.

5
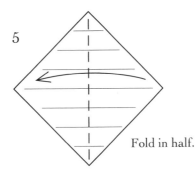
Fold in half.

6
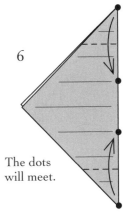
The dots will meet.

7
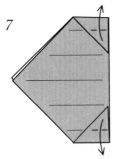
Fold along the creases.

8
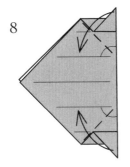

9
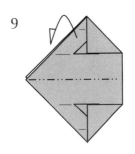
Fold behind.

10
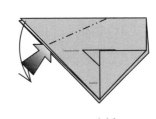
Reverse-fold.

11
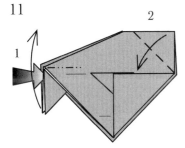
1. Reverse-fold the inner flap.
2. Valley-fold.

12
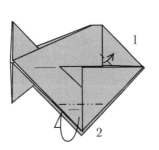
1. Fold the eye.
2. Fold behind, repeat behind.

13
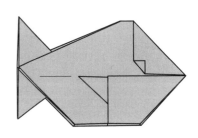
Fish

Crane

1

Fold and unfold.

2

Fold opposite
sides to the center.

3

Fold to the center.

4

Fold behind.

5

Fold the top layer.

6

Squash-fold.

7

Fold behind
and rotate.

8

Reverse-fold and
rotate 180°.

9

Make reverse
folds.

10

Fold inside, repeat behind.

11

Reverse-fold and
spread the wings.

12

Crane

Swan

1

Fold and unfold.

2

Fold to the center.

3

Unfold.

4

5

6

Make squash folds.

7

8

Fold to the center.

9

10

Fold a bit lower.

11

Fold up.

12

Fold in half and rotate.

13

Slide the neck and head.

14

Swan

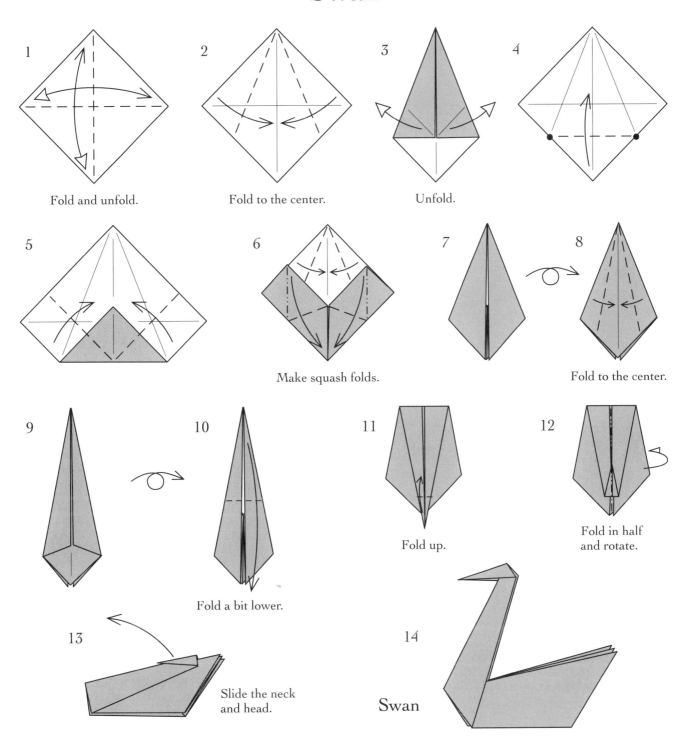

Peacock

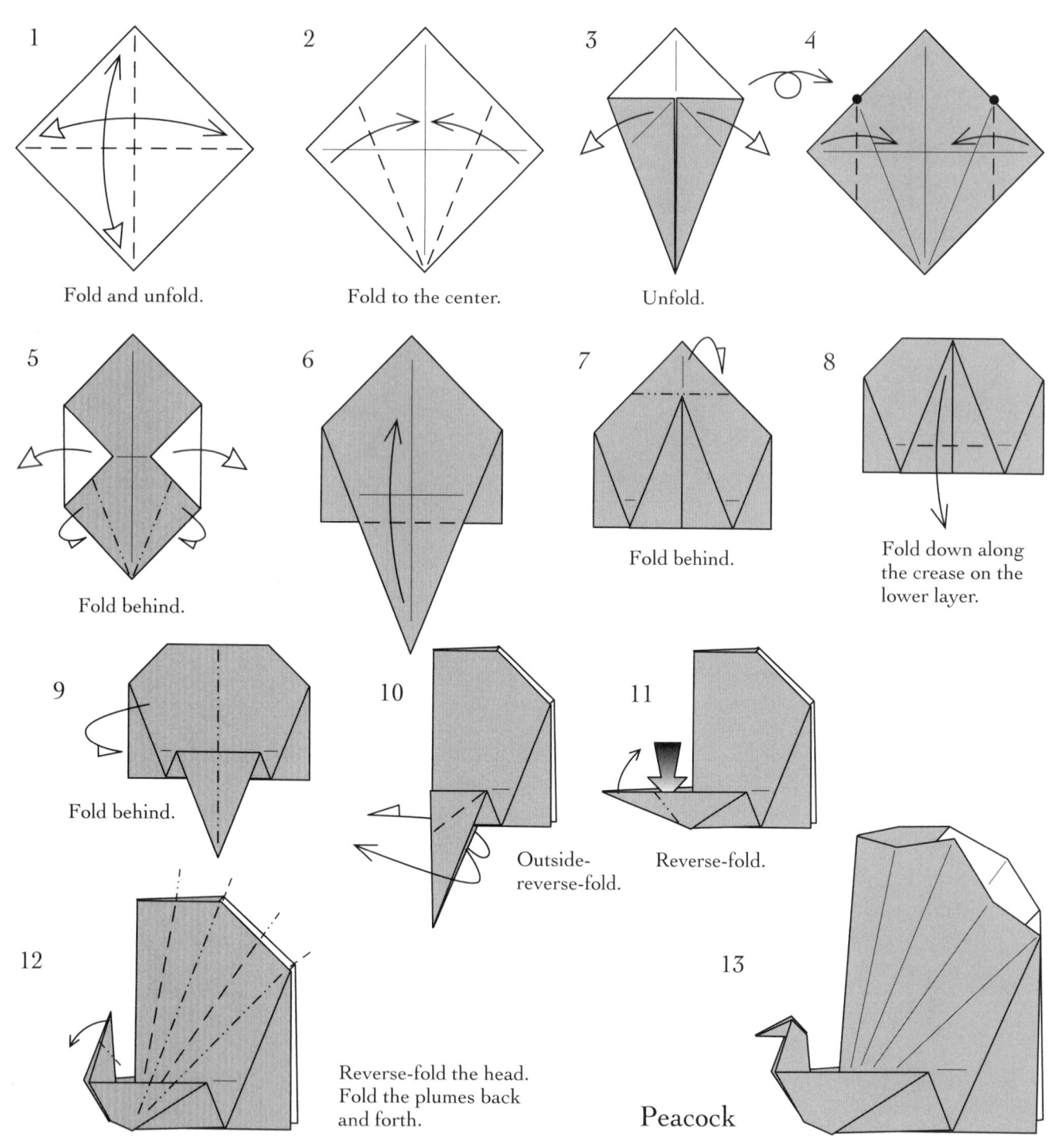

1

Fold and unfold.

2

Fold to the center.

3

Unfold.

4

5

Fold behind.

6

7

Fold behind.

8

Fold down along
the crease on the
lower layer.

9

Fold behind.

10

Outside-
reverse-fold.

11

Reverse-fold.

12

Reverse-fold the head.
Fold the plumes back
and forth.

13

Peacock

Heart

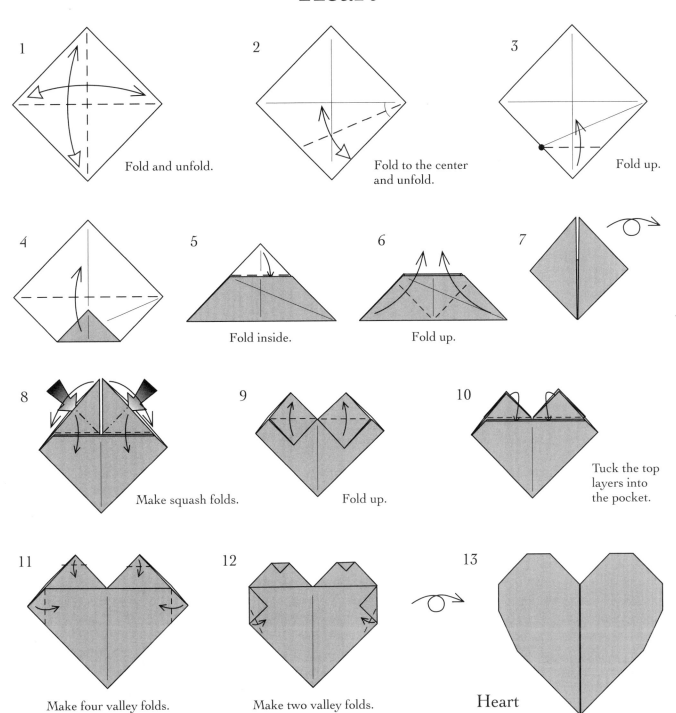

1 Fold and unfold.

2 Fold to the center and unfold.

3 Fold up.

4

5 Fold inside.

6 Fold up.

7

8 Make squash folds.

9 Fold up.

10 Tuck the top layers into the pocket.

11 Make four valley folds.

12 Make two valley folds.

13 Heart

Rose

1

Fold and unfold.

2

Fold the corners to the center.

3

Rotate.

4

Fold to the center and swing out from behind. Rotate.

5

Fold to the center and swing out from behind.

6

Pull out the hidden corner.

7

Pull out three hidden corners.

8

Squash-fold.

9

Make three squash folds.

10

Fold behind so the dots meet.

11

12

The petals lift up a little bit.

13

Rose

Unicorn

1

Fold in half.

2
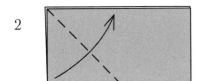

3
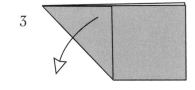

Unfold.

4

Reverse-fold.

5
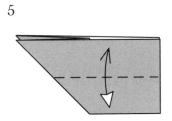

Fold and unfold
all the layers.

6
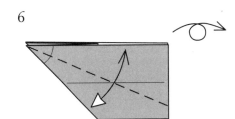

Fold and unfold
all the layers.

7
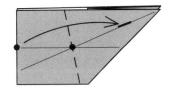

Fold through the intersection
so the dot on the left meets
the bold line on the right.

8
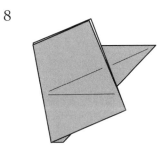

Turn over and rotate 180°.

9
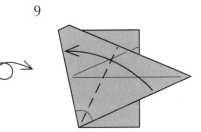

Bisect the angle.

10

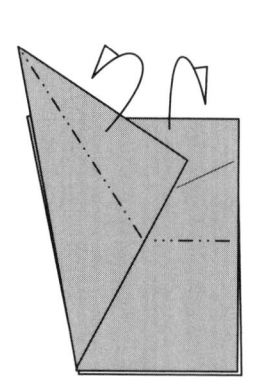

Fold behind
along the creases.

11

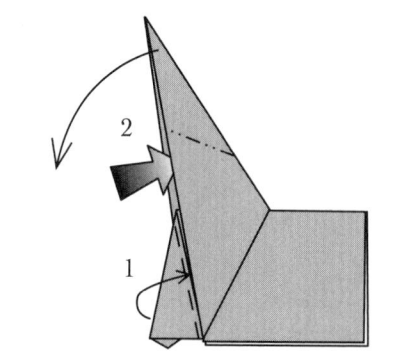
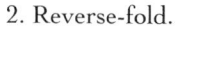

1. Fold inside.
2. Reverse-fold.

12

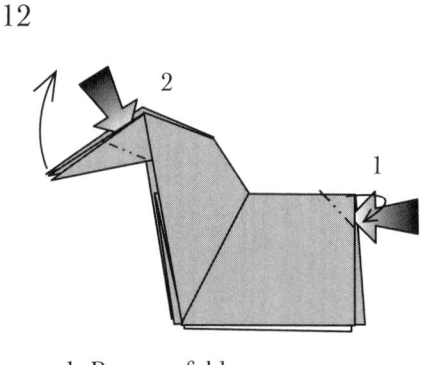

1. Reverse-fold.
2. Reverse-fold the inner flap.

13

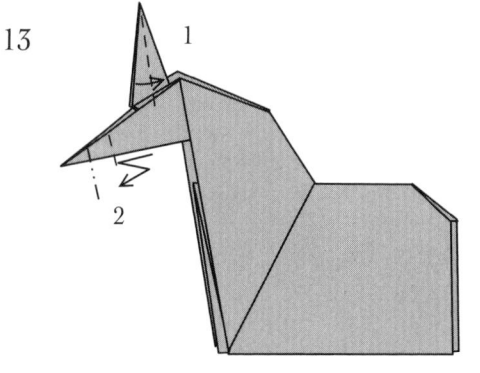

1. Fold in half, repeat behind.
2. Crimp-fold.

14

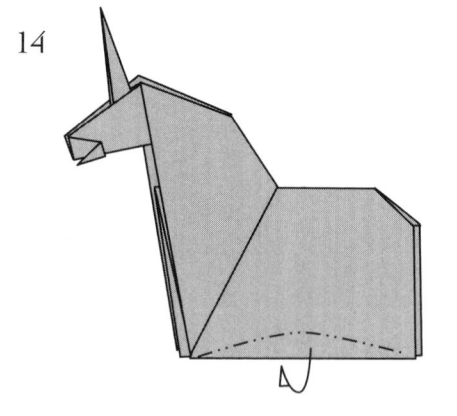

Shape the body and
legs, repeat behind.

15

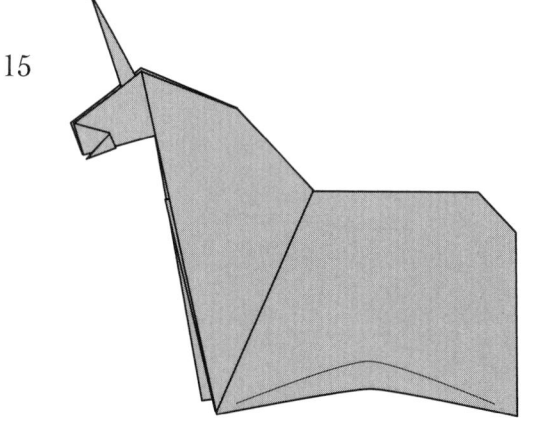

Unicorn

You can't have a positive life with a negative mind.

Just push pause.

Enjoy this moment.

This is the beginning of anything you want.

Nothing can bring you peace but yourself.

When one door closes a window opens.

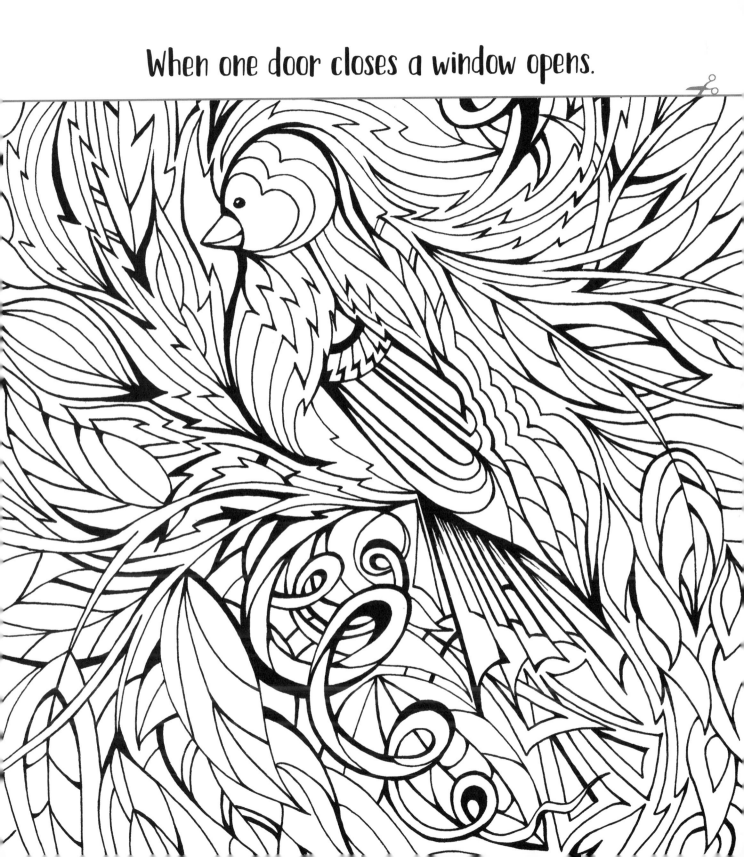

Focus on the journey, not the destination.

Just let it go.

Anything that costs you your peace is too expensive.

Be still.

Knowing yourself is the beginning of all wisdom.

Concentrate the mind on the present moment.

Surrender to what is.

Allow yourself to be.

Each day provides its own gifts.

With our thoughts we make the world.

Nothing is forever except change.

Keep your face to the sunshine and you cannot see a shadow.

Be. Here. Now.